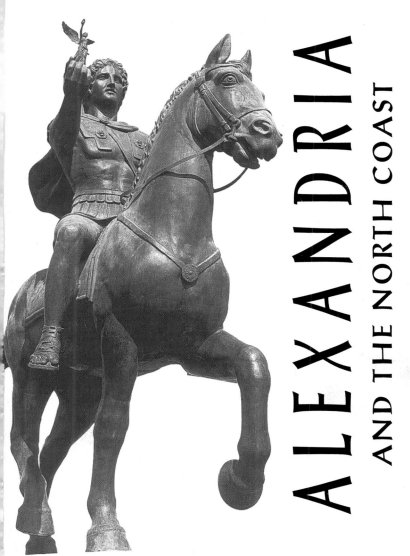

ALEXANDRIA
AND THE NORTH COAST

EGYPT
POCKET
GUIDE

Siliotti

THE AMERICAN UNIVERSITY IN CAIRO PRESS

Text *and Photographs* Alberto Siliotti
...wings Stefania Cossu
...lish Translation Richard Pierce

General Editing Yvonne Marzoni
Graphic Design Geodia

...pyright © 2002 by Geodia (Verona, Italy)

...s edition first published in Egypt jointly by
...e American University in Cairo Press (Cairo and New York)
...s Modern Publishing House (Cairo)
...odia (Verona, Italy)

...eated by Geodia (Verona, Italy)
...nted in Egypt by Elias Modern Publishing House (Cairo)
...tributed by the American University in Cairo Press (Cairo and New York)

...N 977 424 638 1   Dar El Kutub 17878/00

In the text "(⇨ X)" means "go to page X"

Contents

331 BC	Foundation of Alexandria
323	Alexander the Great dies in Babylon
305	Ptolemy, the son of Lagus, one of Alexander's generals, proclaims himself King of Egypt, Ptolemy I
297	Construction of the lighthouse of Alexandria begins
295	Foundation of the library of Alexandria
70	Birth of Cleopatra VII
48	Pompey killed at Pelusium, on the eastern Delta Cleopatra VII meets Julius Caesar at Alexandria
47	Cleopatra marries her brother, Ptolemy XIV First probable fire strikes the library of Alexandria
44	Caesar assassinated in Rome
41	Cleopatra meets Marc Antony at Tarsus, in Cilicia
31	Octavian defeats Marc Antony's fleet in the Battle of Actium
30	Marc Antony and Cleopatra commit suicide End of the Ptolemaic dynasty Egypt becomes a Roman province and remains in Roman sphere of influence for six centuries
642 AD	Amr Ibn al-As, Caliph Omar's emissary, conquers Alexandria The Alexandrian Library is destroyed
1303	An earthquake causes the lighthouse to collapse

MEDITERRANEAN SEA

Pharos Island — Lighthouse of Alexandria

Anfushi Necropolis

Heptastadion (ancient avenue to Pharos Island)

Antirrhodos Island

Center of the ancient city

Necropolis

Rakotis

Kom al-Dikka

Shatbi Necropolis

City wall during first Roman period

Pompey's Pillar Serapeum

Kom al-Shuqafa

Necropolis

MARIUT LAKE (Mareotis)

Modern structures   Ancient structures

Ancient Alexandria

*F*ounded by Alexander the Great in 332 BC, Alexandria soon found its true vocation, becoming the cultural center of the Mediterranean region.

Coin with a portrait of Cleopatra VII (British Museum, London)

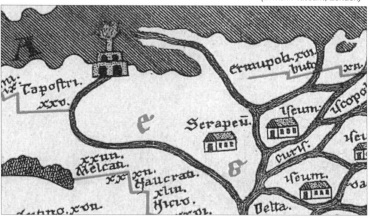

Alexandria and its famous lighthouse in a detail from the Tabula Peutingeriana, the only surviving Roman-period map

Alexandria was founded in 332 BC by Alexander the Great, then 24 years old, and is one of the 34 cities named after the great conqueror. The new city lay in the western part of the Nile River Delta, near the small Egyptian village of Rakotis on the thin strip of land between the Mediterranean Sea and the vast lagoon area that is now Lake Mariut. In the new city, designed by the architect Deinokrates, Greek culture lived side by side with pharaonic civilization, and the interaction of these two worlds gave rise to a new culture known as "Alexandrian" that quickly spread over the entire Mediterranean area. Alexandria was called the "African Athens" and became the capital of Egypt during the reign of the Ptolemaic dynasty, named after its founder Ptolemy I (305–282 BC), who took power after the death of Alexander the Great. The city retained this role until the death of the last sovereign, Cleopatra VII, in 30 BC, when Egypt became a Roman province.

Bust of Alexander the Great (356–323 BC) (Greco-Roman Museum, Alexandria)

Present-day Alexandria

With a population of over five million, Alexandria is the second largest city in Egypt and the country's leading port, as well as a leading tourist attraction. In summer its beaches are crowded with people from Cairo.

View of the seaside promenade in Alexandria, now known as Sharia 26 July *(Corniche)*

Diodorus Siculus, the Greek historian who visited the city in 59 BC, relates that Alexandria extended for 7 km and had more than 300,000 inhabitants, an enormous number at that time. Now the city population is over five million and its port is becoming one of the most important in the Mediterranean, while large industrial and petro-chemical plants have risen up to the south and west of the city. The historic center still has a wealth of ancient monuments such as the Roman Odeum (⇨ **14**), the Serapeum and Pompey's Pillar (⇨ **12**), and the catacombs of Kom al-Shuqafa (⇨ **16**), as well as Islamic buildings like Fort Qaitbay (⇨ **8**) and the al-Mursi mosque. Another attraction is the city's long beaches, crowded in the summer.

The Abu al-Abbas al-Mursi Mosque, built in 1769 and rebuilt in the 20th centuryn, is one of the city's most famous monuments

Recent Discoveries

*A*lexandria has been the scene of many archaeological excavations in recent years, both on land and in the sea, which have yielded important discoveries.

Underwater digs in the Fort Qaitbay area: an archaeologist is making a drawing of the floral motifs on the capital of a Ptolemaic-era column.

In ancient times Alexandria was situated on the site of the present-day city, but the northernmost section, which had many major public buildings, was affected by subsidence that caused these

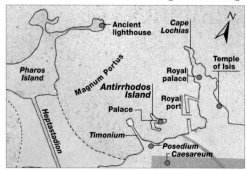

A colossal granite head of a pharaoh from the underwater digs in the Fort Qaitbay area.

monuments to sink into the sea. Many of them were recently found thanks to underwater archaeological excavations. The team headed by the explorer Frank Goddio brought to light the structures that once stood on the island of *Antirrhodos*, which no longer exists, and others in the Abu Qir area (⇨ **32**) further north. The team of the *Centre d'Etudes Alexandrines* (CEA) led by the Egyptologist Jean-Yves Empereur, which is also excavating the site of the ancient lighthouse (⇨ **10**), has carried out a series of excavations in the historic center of the city since 1992, generally when the foundations for new buildings are being laid. These digs have led to important discoveries and have often meant saving precious finds from certain destruction.

Jean-Yves Empereur

Qaitbay Fort

*T*he fort of Sultan Qaitbay is one of the symbols of Alexandria. It was built on the ancient island of Pharos, over the ruins of the world-famous lighthouse.

Medallion commemorating Sultan Qaitbay

The massive Fort Qaitbay on the island of Pharos

In 1477–80, the massive fort that still towers over the entrance to the so-called Eastern Harbor was built at the behest of the Mamluk sultan, Qaitbay (1468–98). It stood on

Detail of the portal of the fort with two commemorative medallions.

what was once the island of Pharos—which was linked to the mainland by a large dam known as the *Heptastadion* since it was seven stadia long (1 stadium is 165 meters)—precisely over the site of the famous lighthouse. The fort was built to provide more efficient defense of the port entrance and of Alexandria itself from Turkish attacks. The building material used consisted of blocks of stone from the lighthouse, which had

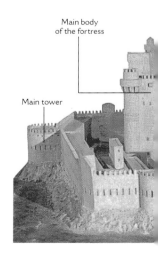

Main body of the fortress

Main tower

almost completely collapsed in August 1303 because of an earthquake and tidal wave, which were followed by another quake in 1326. However, the fort we see today is the result of building ordered by the pasha of Egypt, Muhammad Ali, in the first half of the 19th century; the restoration affected after the English bombardment of Alexandria in 1882, which caused severe damage; and lastly the restoration work carried out in 1984 by the Egyptian Antiquities Organization. The main body of the structure is square, with four massive towers, one at each corner. In the middle is a Cairene-style mosque-madrasa with a cross-shaped plan that is the oldest mosque in Alexandria, and whose vertical axis seems to correspond to that of the ancient lighthouse.

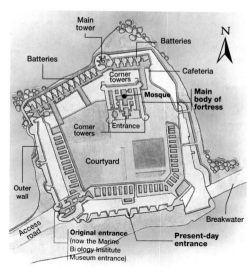

Plan of the Qaitbay Fort

The mosque was originally flanked by a minaret that later collapsed. This square main body is surrounded by a majestic pentagonal wall which is defended by semicircular towers placed at regular intervals, the whole constituting the fortress

A model of the Qaitbay complex and the Naval Museum

proper. On the north side of the wall one can see the batteries that defended access to the port. Originally, the fort entrance was the door flanked by two large round towers that was situated in the southwest corner. The fort is now the home of the **Naval Museum**, which has many finds from the remains of the French fleet destroyed in 1798 by the British under Admiral Horatio Nelson in the famous battle of Abu Qir on exhibit (⇨ **32**). Next to the original entrance is the small **Marine Biology Institute Museum**, with an exhibit of fauna from the Mediterranean Sea, the Red Sea, and the Nile.

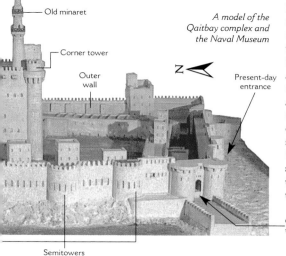

The Lighthouse of Alexandria

The lighthouse, together with the equally famous library, is a symbol of ancient Alexandria. The discovery of part of the lighthouse and the ongoing excavations in the sea opposite the Qaitbay Fort have shed new light on this mythical monument.

Above: the pharos of Abusir, presumably a miniature replica of the one in Alexandria. Top, a 12th-century Arab manuscript illustration of the statue on the top of the Alexandria pharos (Paris, Bibliothèque Nationale)

U sing documents and other historic sources, the German archaeologist Hermann Thiersch was the first to reconstruct, in his famous

Second-century AD coin showing the lighthouse (Paris, Bibliothèque Nationale)

work *Pharos, Antike Islam und Occident* (1909), the famous lighthouse of Alexandria, a monument that already in antiquity was so famous that it was considered one of the Seven Wonders of the Ancient World, the celebrated classification compiled in Alexandria. The lighthouse was named after the place where it was erected, the island of Pharos, a word still used to define this structure that provides warning and guidance to ships entering a port. The construction of this

architectural masterpiece, the work of the architect Sosistratos of Knidos, began around 297 BC under the reign of Ptolemy II and lasted about 15 years. The pharos was 135 meters high and consisted of three stories, on the last of which

stood the gigantic cylindrical lantern which was said to project its light for 50 kilometers.

St. Mark's Basilica, Venice: the pharos of Alexandria in a mosaic

Above the lantern was a dome, which in turn was surmounted by a large statue that perhaps represented

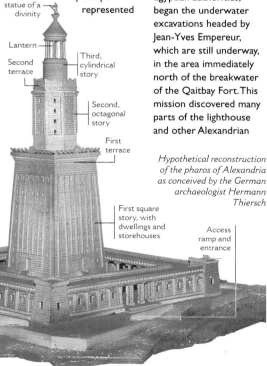

Colossal statue of a divinity

Lantern

Second terrace

Third, cylindrical story

Second, octagonal story

First terrace

First square story, with dwellings and storehouses

Access ramp and entrance

Hypothetical reconstruction of the pharos of Alexandria as conceived by the German archaeologist Hermann Thiersch

Zeus Soter, as the ancient Greek poet Posidippos of Pella said, or Poseidon, the god of the sea. The lighthouse continued to shine for over 15 centuries and was described by numerous Arab and European travelers in the Middle Ages; it is also represented in the mosaics decorating St. Mark's Basilica in Venice. The monument probably began to deteriorate irreversibly in the tenth century because of subsidence and earthquakes, including the one in 1303, which proved to be fatal. In 1994 the CEA, together with the competent Egyptian authorities, began the underwater excavations headed by Jean-Yves Empereur, which are still underway, in the area immediately north of the breakwater of the Qaitbay Fort. This mission discovered many parts of the lighthouse and other Alexandrian

This second-century BC terracotta lantern is a reproduction of the pharos of Alexandria (Greco-Roman Museum, Alexandria)

monuments that comprise a total of over 5,000 blocks dating from both the pharaonic and Greco-Roman periods that were scattered over an area of more than two hectares and at an average of ten meters below sea level. In particular, archaeologists have found some gigantic blocks weighing over 70 tons and have recovered many sphinxes, columns, and the 4.5 meter high bust of a colossal statue of a Ptolemaic pharaoh. Some of these finds are now on exhibit in the garden of the Roman theater of Kom al-Dikka.

THE LIGHTHOUSE IN FIGURES

Original height: 135 m
Time needed for construction: about 15 years
Beginning of construction: 297 BC
Year of inauguration: 282 BC
Visibility: 50 kilometers
Years in use: about 1,585
Year of collapse: 1303

The Serapeum and Pompey's Pillar

*O*n the site of the ancient Temple of Serapis is the tall column erroneously attributed to Pompey.

Statue of the god Serapis
(Greco-Roman Museum,
Alexandria)

Map of Alexandria

C2

The famous Pompey's Pillar towers over the gardens of the Serapeum

Serapis was a syncretic divinity created during the reign of Ptolemy I (305-282 BC), who merged the cult of Osiris with that of the sacred bull Apis and Greek gods such as Zeus, Aclepius, and Dionysus. The cult center of Serapis (an abbreviated form of *Osorapis*) was in Alexandria, where the temple dedicated to this god stood in the Serapeum. This complex lay on a hill in the southwestern section of the city, where the Egyptian quarter of *Rakotis* stood, and housed the necropolis of the sacred bulls of Apis, which were considered reincarnations of the gods Ptah and Osiris. The discovery of a subterranean chamber in the Serapeum in Alexandria, inside which archaeologists found a large statue of the bull Apis (now on exhibit at the Greco-Roman Museum), attests to the existence, even in the

Reconstruction of the Temple of Serapis precinct

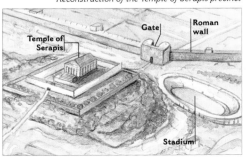

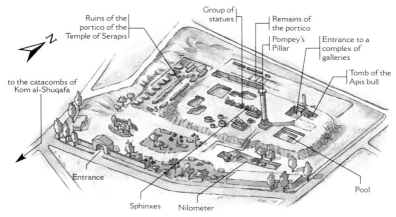

to the catacombs of Kom al-Shuqafa

Ruins of the portico of the Temple of Serapis

Group of statues

Remains of the portico

Pompey's Pillar

Entrance to a complex of galleries

Tomb of the Apis bull

Entrance

Sphinxes

Nilometer

Pool

The Serapeum complex as it is today

Ptolemaic period, of this cult which dates back to

Third-century BC plaque in two languages commemorating the foundation of the Serapeum (Greco-Roman Museum, Alexandria)

the Old Kingdom. As for the Temple of Serapis, the original one built in Ptolemy I's time was replaced by a newer construction during the reign of Ptolemy III (246–222 BC), the only

The capital of Pompey's Pillar

remains of which is a gold plaque commemorating the foundation. Inside this rather small tetrastyle temple (its length was no more than 22 meters) surrounded by the sacred enclosure or precinct (*temenos*), was a statue of the god in the guise of Zeus, the supreme Greek god. Today the Serapeum complex, which was sacked and destroyed by Christians in 391 AD, is occupied by a large garden with many archaeological finds, the most important of which is the famous Pompey's Pillar, 30 meters high (98 feet) and with a circumference of nine meters. This column, carved out of a block of red granite, was erected in 298 AD by Publius, the prefect of Egypt, in honor of the Roman emperor Diocletian, as can be seen in the Greek inscription carved on the west side of the base of this monument—there is no historical foundation

The so-called tomb of the Apis bull in the Serapeum garden

whatsoever for its being named after Pompey. Flanking the pillar are two pink granite sphinxes that were found not far away in 1906.

One of the two sphinxes flanking Pompey's Pillar

The Roman Odeum

*T*he small Roman odeum at Kom al-Dikka dates from the 4th century AD and originally had a roof. Its tiers could accommodate 600 spectators.

A marble mask

Map of Alexandria

C4

The Roman odeum at Kom al-Dikka

Surrounded by greenery even though it lies in the heart of town, the small odeum of Kom al-Dikka, which in Arabic means "hill of

Detail of the portico near the odeum

rubble," is commonly known as the Roman Theater. The odeum was brought to light from 1960 to 1965 by archaeologists from the University of Warsaw. The odeum we see today dates from the 4th century AD and is the only existing example in Egypt of this type of building, which was so characteristic of the Greco-Roman period. Odea are a special kind of roofed theater used for music and poetry competitions.

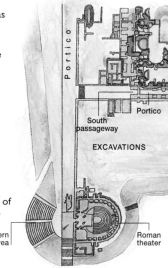

Portico

Portico

South passageway

EXCAVATIONS

Modern cavea

Roman theater

The cavea of the Alexandrian odeum, which could seat about 600 persons, is semicircular with extended wings; it has a diameter of 33 meters and consists of 13 tiers made of European white marble; in the uppermost section is a portico with Aswan granite columns, some of which are still standing. The odeum was destroyed by an earthquake in the sixth or seventh century. North of the theater, opposite which is a modern cavea used for spectacles during the summer, are the large brick structures corresponding to the second to fourth century AD baths.

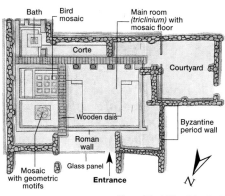

Plan of the Villa of the Birds

The Villa of the Birds

East of the odeum, recent digs have brought to light a Roman villa dating from the reign of Hadrian (second century AD) that archaeologists

decoration in this villa has geometric motifs executed with the *opus tessellatum* technique, in which patterns are formed by small, multicolored cubes of exactly same size, known as *tesserae*.

The Villa of the Birds is the most beautiful example of a private Roman house in Alexandria and its fine state of preservation is under the protection of the Egyptian Supreme Council of Antiquities (SCA) and the American Research Center in Egypt.

Details of the mosaic floor in the Villa of the Birds

have named the Villa of the Birds because of the splendid mosaic floor in the main room (the *triclinium*) depicting many magnificent birds using the *opus sectile* technique, which calls for slabs of marble or other material cut into pieces of various shapes to follow the outline of the images. Other mosaic

This sphinx is one of the many found during the underwater excavations at Fort Qaitbay in Alexandria. They are now on exhibit in the Kom al-Dikka garden

Plan of the Kom al-Dikka archaeological precinct

The Catacombs of Kom al-Shuqafa

The most important hypogeum in Alexandria, the Kom al-Shuqafa catacombs date from the 2nd century AD and their decoration is the result of the fusion of Hellenistic and pharaonic elements so typical of Alexandrian art and culture.

Map of Alexandria

C2

The façade of the main tomb at Kom al-Shuqafa

The catacombs of Kom al-Shuqafa, the "hill of treasures," were discovered by chance in 1900. In rock-hewn ground under the city, these catacombs are laid out on three levels, access to which is afforded by a spiral stairway winding around a large **central shaft** used both for transporting the dead to their graves and for ensuring ventilation in the chambers. The central shaft communicates, via a vestibule, with a **rotunda** that in turn leads to the *triclinium*, which was used for the funerary banquets in honor of the deceased that took place on special days considered holy by the cult. Along the walls of the *triclinium* are three benches cut out of the rock in a "U" shape around the middle of the hall where a wooden table must have stood. To the west of the rotunda and *triclinium* is the complex of **galleries**, on the walls of which are the loculi where the deceased were placed. East of the rotunda is a tomb that is totally independent from the rest of the complex; here lies the **Hall of Caracalla**, so named because, according to tradition, the remains of the young Alexandrian

Bas-relief of Agathodaimon, the tutelary divinity of Alexandria

The deep central shaft around which the access stairway winds

rotunda to the **main tomb** in the necropolis, which is the most interesting part of the catacombs. This tomb dates back to the period of the emperors Domitian and Trajan (81–138 AD) and is in fact decorated with statues and bas-reliefs in which the classical funerary motifs of pharaonic Egypt are rendered in keeping with Greco-Roman canons. In like manner the symbolism used combines typically Egyptian

elements such as the winged sun disk of the god Horus or the double crown of Upper and Lower Egypt with Greek symbols such as the thyrsus (a pine cone-tipped staff) connected to the Dionysian cult or the caduceus (a staff with entwined snakes and a pair of wings at the top) of the god Hermes. The tomb includes a vast antechamber in the middle of which is a tunnel (**A**) leading to the third level of the

Christians who were massacred at the behest of the Roman emperor in 215 AD supposedly lie there. It must be said that the tradition concerning this tomb has no historical basis, since the numerous bones found in this area were found to be those of horses, which were presumably buried here intentionally. A stairway leads from the

One of the many galleries with loculi in the catacombs

First level tombs

Caracalla section (hypogeum 2)

Original structure of the main tomb on 2nd level (hypogeum 1)

Tombs added on the second level

The complex plan of the Kom al-Shuqafa catacombs

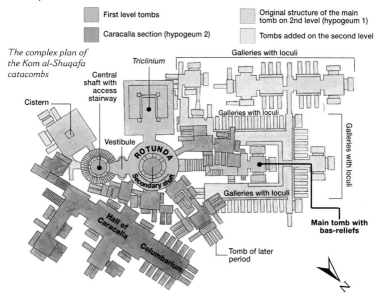

Cistern

Triclinium

Central shaft with access stairway

Galleries with loculi

Vestibule

ROTUNDA

Secondary shaft

Galleries with loculi

Galleries with loculi

Galleries with loculi

Galleries with loculi

Hall of Caracalla

Columbarium

Tomb of later period

Main tomb with bas-reliefs

N

The main sarcophagus in the tomb in the burial chamber, ornamented with garlands and Medusa heads. On either side of the deceased lying on the funerary bed are Osiris (left) and a priest in charge of the burial ritual (right)

This Greco-Roman style statue of an unidentified man stands in one of the two niches at the sides of the door leading to the burial chamber

catacombs, which is inaccessible because it is filled with water from the underground water table. At the back end are two columns whose capitals are decorated with lotus and papyrus motifs above which is the classical winged sun disk of the god Horus that protects the tomb. At either side of the door to the burial chamber are bas-reliefs of sacred cobras (**B**) that also have a protective function and are to be identified as the

The bas-relief above one of the side sarcophagi in the burial chamber. It represents the sacred bull Apis before the emperor, while a goddess (probably Isis or Hathor) spreads her wings to protect him

Inside the burial chamber are two reliefs of Anubis, the god of the dead, in the guise of a Roman legionary

Agathodaimon, the syncretic tutelary divinity of Alexandria. On the side walls of the antechamber are two niches (**C**) with the statues, without inscriptions, of a man (right) and woman (left), who may represent the couple for whom this tomb was made or their children. The burial chamber (**D**) has a sarcophagus in the middle that probably belongs to a woman, and two other side sarcophagi; all three are decorated with floral garlands and above them are reliefs that clearly reveal the above-mentioned mixture of Egyptian and Greco-Roman elements. On the inner sides of the door are two reliefs of the god Anubis dressed like a Roman legionary.

One of the most important paintings in the Tigrane tomb depicts the deceased in the guise of Osiris on his funerary couch between the goddesses Isis and Nephthys, who are holding palm branches

The Tigrane Tomb and the Wardian Tomb

A few dozen meters from the entrance to the Kom al-Shuqafa catacombs, the Tigrane tomb is known for the paintings on the walls in which pharaonic funerary motifs are

Floral and plant motifs predominate in the wall decoration

mixed with others of Greek derivation and executed in the typical Alexandrian Hellenistic style.

This tomb, which dates from the late 1st century AD, was discovered in 1952 in a necropolis situated in Tigrane Pasha Street (now Port Said Street) and then transported to its present location a few meters from the so-called Wardian Tomb, which comes from the Wardian area in the western necropolis complex.

This latter tomb was reconstructed; it consists of a small painted chapel that once

Detail of the ceiling decoration in the Tigrane tomb with the head of Medusa

housed the statue of a goddess, perhaps identifiable as Isis.

The so-called Wardian Tomb

The Necropolis of Anfushi

A nfushi belongs to the group of western necropoli and is characterized by tombs whose walls are decorated with geometric motifs.

The entrance to the Anfushi necropolis

S ituated in the Ras al-Tin peninsula, Anfushi is one of the western necropoli. Five tombs were discovered there in 1901 and 1921 dating from the first half of the 3rd century AD.
The most interesting of these is Tomb 1.
A rock-hewn stairway leads to an open courtyard surrounded by several chambers. A long vestibule with benches cut out of the rock precedes the burial chamber, which contains a large sarcophagus made of pink Aswan granite. The walls are stuccoed and painted to represent imitation marble and alabaster, while the ceiling of the burial chamber is vaulted and decorated with geometric motifs that characterize the decorative scheme of this tomb, the walls of which are ornamented with white, black, blue, or red squares, lozenges, and octagons, creating *trompe l'œil* cornices and coffers.

The burial chamber of Tomb 1, decorated with polychrome geometric motifs

Plan of Tomb 1

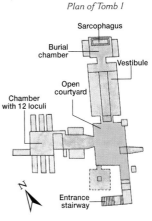

Sarcophagus

Burial chamber

Vestibule

Open courtyard

Chamber with 12 loculi

Entrance stairway

N

The Necropolis of Mustafa Kamil

This small necropolis discovered in the 1930s is interesting for the monumentality and elegance of its tombs, one of which is decorated with a polychrome frieze depicting a libation scene with ladies-in-waiting and horsemen.

B6

Map of Alexandria

The south wall of the courtyard in Tomb 1, decorated with Doric columns and six small sphinxes. In the middle is an altar. The arrow indicates the frieze with the libation scene

The necropolis of Mustafa Kamil, like the Shatbi necropolis (⇨ **22**), is part of the group of eastern necropoli and comprises two tombs discovered in 1933–34

Plan of tomb 1

N

Doric columns — Access stairway

Transverse vestibule

Altar

Chambers with loculi

Well

Cisterns

Roofless central courtyard — Chambers with loculi

dating from the end of the 3rd century AD. Tomb 1, the most impressive one, consists of a large roofless courtyard reached by means of a stairway, much like the main tomb at Anfushi (⇨ **20**). In the middle of the courtyard is an altar facing the south wall, which was originally decorated with six small sphinxes and which has three doors giving access to the transverse vestibule. Above the central door, which is flanked by two Doric columns, is a beautiful polychrome painting of a

libation scene with three horsemen in uniform holding a vase, while two women are making offerings. In the middle of

Polychrome frieze with horsemen and a libation scene

the opposite wall is a cistern fed by a well in a side chamber to the west.

The Necropolis of Shatbi

*S*ituated a short distance from the sea, the necropolis of Shatbi is the most ancient one in Alexandria and has yielded many important finds that are now in the city's Greco-Roman Museum.

Polychrome terracotta statue

Map of Alexandria

B5

*S*habti is an ancient necropolis dating from the 3rd century BC where excavations have unearthed a great many valuable finds that are now in the Greco-Roman Museum, in particular the famous, elegant, polychrome terracotta statuettes of two richly dressed Alexandrian ladies. The tombs in this necropolis have no decoration, and their interest lies in the architectural style, since the main one was modeled after a typical Greek house. This type of tomb is therefore called *oikos*. It is laid out on a longitudinal axis along which are the various characteristic Hellenistic structural elements: the open courtyard, the vestibule and the alcove, which is the burial chamber representing the *oikos* and is the focal point of the entire complex.

View of the necropolis of Shatbi

Plan of the main tomb of Shatbi

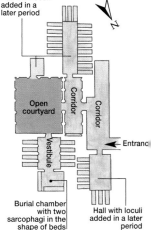

Hall with loculi added in a later period

N

Open courtyard

Corridor

Corridor

Vestibule

← Entrance

Burial chamber with two sarcophagi in the shape of beds

Hall with loculi added in a later period

The main tomb of Shatbi, which is now flooded

The Greco-Roman Museum

This museum, founded in 1895 by the Italian archaeologist Giuseppe Botti, is a veritable monument to Alexandrian culture.

The Neoclassic façade of the Greco-Roman Museum

B4

Map of Alexandria

The Greco-Roman Museum boasts the most important collections of finds related to Alexandrian civilization and is a treasure trove for scholars and enthusiasts

One of the museum corridors

of this cultural world, in which thousands of years of pharaonic Egyptian civilization merged with the ancient Greek and Roman cultures. In 1894 the last khedive of Egypt, Abbas II, decided to found a large museum to commemorate the splendor of the city's glorious past. He gave the Italian archaeologist Giuseppe Botti, who had already founded a small private museum in 1891, the opportunity to place his collections in a more prestigious site. The museum collection soon grew in size, thanks to the donations of many private collectors and to the excavations carried out by Botti, the first museum director, and his two successors, who

continued his research: Evaristo Breccia and Achille Adriani, the latter holding this position until 1952.

The museum, built in 1895 in Neoclassic style, has 27 rooms and an elegant garden in which many finds are exhibited: sarcophagi, statues, stelae, and a small second-century BC

The Italian archaeologist Giuseppe Botti (1853–1903), founder and first director of the Greco-Roman Museum

The museum garden has many interesting inscriptions on display

Detail of the mosaic by Sophilos (3rd century BC) portraying Berenice II

temple dedicated to the crocodile god Sobek from the ancient city of *Theadelphia* in the Fayum. In fact, the finds on display do not come from the Alexandria region alone, but from all of Egypt in order to provide the best representation of the historic periods covered by the museum. The institution is divided into various sections that include finds from different periods of Egypt's history. Rooms 1 and 2, in the south wing, have Early Christian finds: marble bas-reliefs, statues, and a famous relief of St. Menas flanked

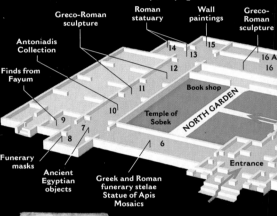

Greco-Roman sculpture

Antoniadis Collection

Finds from Fayum

Roman statuary

Wall paintings

Greco-Roman sculpture

14   13   15

16 A

12   16

11

Book shop

10

NORTH GARDEN

Temple of Sobek

9   7

8   6

Funerary masks

Ancient Egyptian objects

Greek and Roman funerary stelae Statue of Apis Mosaics

Entrance

A second-century BC silver chalice with Cupid and Dionysus (Room 3)

Bas-relief of St. Menas (fifth century AD)

foundation of the Serapeum (⇨ **32**). Rooms 4 and 5 have examples of Coptic art (textiles, wall paintings, funerary stelae). Room 6,

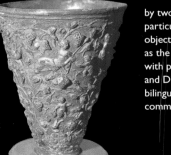

by two camels. There are particularly precious objects in Room 3, such as the gilded silver chalice with portrayals of Cupid and Dionysus, and the bilingual gold tablets commemorating the

Fifth-century AD wall painting of the Archangel Gabriel (Room 5)

View of Room 6: in the middle is the statue of the sacred bull Apis, and at left Sophilos' mosaic

objects from the pharaonic period, most of which were brought to light during the digs at Abu Qir, while the next room (8) displays some beautiful funerary masks in painted plaster. Room 9 contains finds from the excavations at *Theadelphia* (Fayum), including a crocodile mummy. Various items from the Antoniadis Collection are in Room 10, and Room 11 has Greco-Roman finds on exhibit, including a small funerary stela portraying

Plan of the Greco-Roman Museum

Roman sculpture Sarcophagi

Tanagra terracottas

Greco-Roman funerary finds Terracotta

Grave goods

17

18A
18

Library

20

19

21

23
Bronze objects

22

SOUTH GARDEN

24
Coins

Glass objects

Offices

1

3

Jewelry

N

2

4

5

Early Christian finds

Coptic art

Funerary stela (third century BC) of a Macedonian horseman (Room 11)

in the north wing, contains Greco-Roman epigraphs; a famous basalt

statue of the sacred bull Apis; a large second-century BC mosaic from the Delta by the Greek artist Sophilos with a portrait of Berenice II, the wife of Ptolemy III; and a marble bust of Alexander the Great. In Room 7 are

a Macedonian horseman. Statuary of this period is on exhibit in Room 12, including an elegant statue of Marcus Aurelius, who visited Alexandria in 175 AD.

Basalt statue of Apis (120 BC) found in a subterranean chamber of the Serapeum (Room 6)

Marble bust of Augustus (Room 13)

Wall painting representing a sakia, *or hydraulic wheel, from the west necropolis. This is one of the most beautiful pieces in the museum (Room 15)*

Other Roman statues are displayed in Rooms 13 and 14; these include four headless statues of orators and two beautiful marble busts of Julius Caesar and Augustus. In Room 15 visitors can admire a splendid wall painting, probably dating from the second century BC, that was found in the necroplis area of

Polychrome Tanagra terracotta figurines dating from second century BC (Room 18A)

3rd-2nd century BC funerary urns (hydriae) from Hadra (Room 18)

Gabbari, depicting a *sakia* or hydraulic wheel. Greco-Roman sculpture is also exhibited in Rooms 16, 16A, and 17, the last mentioned boasting some fine marble sarcophagi, a

Blue glass duck (second century BC, Room 22)

gigantic headless statue of an emperor, and a second century BC mosaic from the Dakhla oasis depicting a Nilotic banquet.

Rooms 18, 18A, and 19 are given over to terracotta objects; number 18 has a small lantern representing the Alexandria lighthouse (⇨ 12), as well as a collection of funerary urns known as *hydriae*, most of which come from the Hadra necropolis. Of particular interest in Room 18A are the elegant, brightly colored terracotta Tanagra figurines (named after the locality in Boetia, Greece, where they were first discovered) that for the most part represent Alexandrian ladies (3rd-2nd century BC); these were found in the Alexandrian necropoli of Hadra and Shatbi. Again in Room 18A, there is a terracotta bust of Alexander the Great.

Rooms 20 and 21 are given over to grave goods: urns, gilded bronze burial crowns, ceramics, and many terracotta lamps, which was a specialty of Alexandrian craftsmen, who were known throughout the ancient world. Among the most noteworthy objects is a piece of colored glass dating from the first century BC representing a theater mask surrounded by a floral motif typical of the Alexandrian school. Other fine pieces are two small ducks made of blue glass with an

Piece of colored glass with a theater mask (first century BC, Room 22)

extremely elegant shape, and a third-century BC vitreous paste pendant. In Room 23 there are numerous bronze objects, the most fascinating of which is a splendid bust, supposedly of the Emperor Hadrian, that dates back to the second century AD and comes from Qena in Upper Egypt.

Room 24, at the end of the building, can be visited only with special permission from the

Vitreous paste pendant (third century BC, Room 22)

museum management. It boasts a large coin collection of Greek, Roman, Byzantine, and Islamic coins—about 7,000 pieces on display on 255 revolving panels.

Gold octadrachm with portrait of Ptolemy II (285–246 BC, Room 24)

Bronze bust of the emperor Hadrian from Qena (Room 23)

The Bibliotheca Alexandrina

The pride and joy of Alexandria, the Library was once the cultural center of the ancient world. Destroyed in mysterious circumstances, it has found new life thanks to UNESCO.

The Bibliotheca Alexandrina *logo*

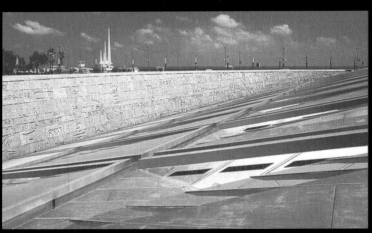

The roof of the library is made of glass panels and steel

The idea of creating a building to house all the writings in the world is probably to be attributed to Ptolemy I, who entrusted this task to Demetrius Phalereus, as "head of the Royal Library," in 295 BC. Demetrius, who had unlimited financial and human resources at his disposal, managed to build the library in a short time. It contained some 500,000 papyrus rolls, representing virtually all human knowledge to that point, and soon became a cultural center that undertook prestigious and complicated initiatives

Third-century BC mosaic of a dog found during the excavation on the site of the new Bibliotheca Alexandrina, in the area of the ancient Ptolemy royal palace

such as translating the Old Testament into Greek as part of a program of systematic translations into Greek of all the major works written in other languages.

The library was built near the Ptolemy royal palace, to which was added an important research center known as the Mouseion. But the number of works soon became so large that an annex had to be built in the Serapeum complex. Famous persons worked in the library: the poet and critic Callimachus; the philospher and mathematician Eratosthenes of Cyrene, who measured the circumference of the Earth with good approximation; the great author Hecateus of Abdera; and the historian Manetho, the priest of Heliopolis who wrote a chronology of Egypt which introduced the concept of dynasties. The library of Alexandria was first damaged by fire in 47 AD and then totally destroyed in 642 when the city was conquered by the Arabs. Many centuries later, the idea of rebuilding this great library began to attract notice, and in 1986 the project involving the Egyptian government, UNESCO and UNDP (United Nations Development Program) finally became operational. More than 500 architects took part in the international competition for the construction of the building, which was won by the Norwegian Snøetta studio. In 1988 the Egyptian president Mubarak laid the first stone along the coast on

View of the Bibliotheca Alexandrina

the Silsila peninsula, which borders the Eastern Harbor to the east, where the ancient Royal Quarter once stood. The *Bibliotheca Alexandrina* was finished in 2000 with the aid and contribution of Arab and European nations and the United States. It covers a surface area of 36,770 square meters and is a truncated cylinder with a diameter of 160 meters and a maximum height of 33 meters. The back, and

highest, section of the library, which is made of Aswan granite, is decorated with the letters of all the languages in the world. The roof consists of a strongly inclined steel frame with special glass panels. The Bibliotheca, which will contain eight million books, will surely become an unprecedented, unique cultural center that once again bears witness to Alexandria's international and cultural vocation.

THE *BIBLIOTHECA ALEXANDRINA* IN FIGURES

Year when construction began: 1988
Year of inauguration: 2000
Number of books it will contain: 8,000,000
Total surface area of complex: 89,540 square meters
Surface area of library: 36,770 square meters
Number of chairs for readers: 2,000
Maximum height of structure: 33 meters
Number of stories: 11, 7 of which will be only for reading
Length of façade: 305 meters
Building cost: $176,000,000

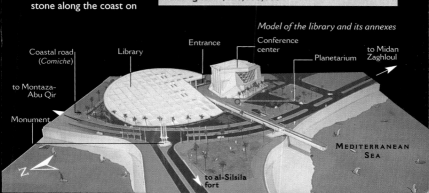

Model of the library and its annexes

Coastal road (Corniche) — Library — Entrance — Conference center — Planetarium — to Midan Zaghloul

to Montaza-Abu Qir

Monument

to al-Silsila fort

MEDITERRANEAN SEA

N

The Royal Jewelry Museum

Map of Alexandria

B6

One of the splendid rooms in the museum

The sumptuous palace that was once the residence of Princess Fatma al-Zahra now houses a collection of precious objects that were part of the royal treasury.

The Royal Jewelry Museum, housed in the former Royal Palace belonging to Princess Fatma al-Zahra, in the Zizinia neighborhood of eastern Alexandria, has a large collection of precious artistic objects that once belonged to the royal treasury. The oldest objects date from the 19th century, during the rule of the viceroy Muhammad Ali (1805-1849). Among the most interesting and valuable is a collection of pocket watches with enamel portraits of the rulers of Egypt, from Muhammad Ali to Said Pasha (1854-1863), and a golden diadem with pearls and

A gold watch with the portrait of Said Pasha

many diamonds. There are also curious pieces such as garden tools decorated with precious stones, and a chess set made of mounted diamonds.

A platinum tiara with 2,159 diamonds that once belonged to the family of King Fuad I

The Montaza Palace and Gardens

*T*he large Montaza Park, situated east of the center of Alexandria, a short distance from Abuqir, has a luxurious Neo-Gothic palace that is now one of the Egyptian president's residences.

The Haramlik Palace at Montaza

*E*ast of Alexandria, at the end of the *Corniche*, the boulevard that runs along the Mediterranean coast, about 20 kilometers from city center, lie the Montaza gardens. This area was chosen by King Fuad (1922–36) as the site of a vast Neo-Gothic summer palace that was finished in 1932 and called *Haramlik*.

The building is now one of the residences of the Egyptian president and is not open to the public.

Detail of the Montaza gardens, which have a surface area of 46 hectares

In 1892, in the same Montaza area, the Khedive Abbas II had had a palace built that was called *Salamlik*. This is much smaller than the other palace and is now a historic hotel that has photographs and memorabilia of the Egyptian royal family on display. In more recent times King Farouk, Fuad's son, had a huge bridge built at Montaza to afford access to an islet with an elegant pavilion where the king himself liked to stay.

Abu Qir

The fort at Abu Qir in a 19th-century engraving

*T*he theater of a great naval battle in 1798, Abu Qir is a well-known seaside town that has yielded many new and important archaeological discoveries.

A fishing boat in Abu Qir Bay

Abu Qir is the name of a promontory with a popular resort town with over 300,000 inhabitants that has been incorporated into the city of Alexandria. This locality

research.

On August 1, 1798, the French fleet, which had arrived in Egypt a short time earlier, was routed by the English navy led by the Admiral Horatio Nelson; and on July 25,

1799 the French troops under General Kleber defeated the Turks of Mustafa Pasha here. Underwater excavations carried out by Franck Goddio's team in the sandy sea floor of the bay

Horatio Nelson, the admiral of the British fleet at Abu Qir

is not only known for two important battles, but for a series of recent archaeological discoveries; furthermore, the area is now the venue of further excavations and

The naval battle of Abu Qir

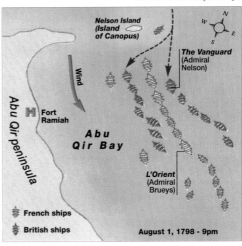

Nelson Island (Island of Canopus)

W　N　E　S

The Vanguard (Admiral Nelson)

Wind

Fort Ramiah

A b u Q i r B a y

L'Orient (Admiral Brueys)

Abu Qir peninsula

French ships
British ships

August 1, 1798 - 9pm

have localized the remains of the French fleet, in particular the admiral ship *L'Orient*, which exploded during the battle, killing 1,500 sailors. Other discoveries made by Goddio in the Abu Qir area concern much earlier periods. Here he found the city of *Canopus*, which was the leading commercial city in Egypt before Alexandria was founded. Its importance lay in the

The head of an ancient Egyptian statue in Abu Qir Bay

Some objects on L'Orient found at the bottom of the bay (Naval Museum, Alexandria)

fact that it sat along an arm of the Nile, known as the Canopic, which was the only watercourse linking the capital, Memphis, with the Mediterranean. In June 2000 Goddio announced he had discovered the ancient cities of Canopus, two kilometers off the Abu Qir coastline, and *Herakleon*, six

kilometers from the coast. Both sites yielded many important archaeological finds. While a part of the site of Canopus had already been found in 1933 by Prince Omar Tussun's mission, which had unearthed a bust of Alexander the Great, Herakleon, which lay precisely at the mouth of the Canopic arm of the Nile, was totally unknown until then.

NELSON ISLAND: DIGS AND DISCOVERIES

Excavations and research are also being carried out on Nelson Island (also known as Canopus Island), two

kilometers from the Abu Qir promontory. This islet, which is only 350 meters long, is being explored

Monumental building

Hellenistic residential area

N

by a team of Italian archaeologists from the University of Turin headed by Paolo Gallo. The mission has also drawn up the first topographical map of the islet and has found a late fourth-century BC Hellenistic settlement.

Rosetta

*T*he city of Rosetta owes its international fame to the discovery of the famous Rosetta Stone, but few people are aware that it has many monuments that are well worth visiting.

View of the city of Rosetta

Rosetta–*Rachid* in Arabic–is a town with 60,000 inhabitants situated 65 kilometers east of Alexandria on the left shore of the west arm of the Nile, which flows into the Mediterranean a few kilometers away. Although this town is known for the famous stela that allowed Champollion to decipher Egyptian hieroglyphs, from an architectural standpoint it is the richest city in the Nile

The interior of the Ramadan House

The mill in the Abu Shahin House

The **Arab Killi House**, formerly the governor's residence, is now the home of the city museum.

There are also two interesting mosques: the 18th-century **Al-Mahalli**, about a hundred meters from the Abu Shahin House, has a ceiling supported by 99 columns from ancient Alexandrian monuments; and **Zaghlul**, the oldest mosque in Rosetta.

River Delta and is virtually unknown to present-day tourists. The narrow streets of its historic center have numerous 16th-18th century private houses and some mosques that are fine examples of Islamic architecture. In the 18th and early 19th century Rosetta was Egypt's leading port until Alexandria supplanted it, and many Europeans considered it one of the most pleasant cities in Egypt.

Among the most important monuments in Rosetta are such private residences as the perfectly restored **Ramadan House**, which some people think is the most beautiful in

town, the **Amasyali House**, and **the Abu Shahin House**, in which

The 18th-century Arab Killi House, now the Municipal Museum

A decorated door in the Ramadan House

a large mill has been reconstructed. All these historic residences have similar features: they are tall, two or three stories high, are made of undressed bricks, have many large windows, and their front doors are large enough to allow a loaded camel to pass through.

The 18th-century public baths, **Hammam Azuz**, have preserved their original architecture. Lastly, in the northern part of town, along the Nile River, is the **Fort of Qaitbay**, entirely restored in the 1980s, where the famous Rosetta Stone was found.

The Rosetta Stone

*I*t was here, in July 1799, that the French Engineer Corps officer Pierre Bouchard happened upon the slab that helped Jean-François Champollion to find the key to solving the mystery of Egyptian hieroglyphs.

View of the fort at Rosetta built in the 15th century by Qaitbay

While the French troops were consolidating the present-day Qaitbay fort—at the time called *Burg Rashid* (the Rosetta Tower) by the locals and then renamed *Fort Julien* by the French—to defend the city from a possible Turkish attack, a large dark stone slab covered with inscriptions was found during the excavation work and attracted the attention of Engineer Corps officer Pierre Bouchard. The mathematician Michal-Ange Lancret, who was at the site, immediately related this discovery to the *Institut d'Egypte* in Cairo, the committee of scientists established by Napoleon, of which

A cast of the Rosetta Stone in the Qaitbay fort

Champollion's Egyptian grammar

The name Ptolemy *in hieroglyphic script*

Text in hieroglyphics

Text in demotic Egyptian

The name Ptolemy *in Greek*

Text in Greek

decided to make reproductions and plaster casts of the slab, which proved to be a wise move, since after the surrender of the French Army this invaluable object fell into the hands of the English, who took it to the British Museum in

Jean-François Champollion 1790-1832

Egyptian demotic, which was the long-awaited key that allowed Jean-François Champollion to unravel the mystery of hieroglyphic writing in 1822.

A few months after the discovery, the Orientalist Jean Michel Marcel had already noted that Ptolemy's name was repeated eleven times, and he tried in vain to find the corresponding hieroglyphic name. Later on, many other scholars also tried to reveal the secret of the stone, but only Champollion succeeded in correctly identifying Ptolemy's name in hieroglyphic script and various other hieroglyphs, thus taking the first step toward decipherment.

Lancret was a member. Bouchard was ordered to transport the precious slab to Cairo. The official announcement of the find was given on July 29, 1799 during one of the periodic meetings of the *Institut d'Egypte*. It was London, where it is still kept. The writing on the dark granite tablet was a decree that Ptolemy V (205-180 BC) had issued in 196 AD in Greek, Egyptian hieroglyphs, and

THE ROSETTA STONE IN FIGURES

Weight: 762 kg
Length: 114 cm
Width: 72 cm
Average thickness: 27 cm

Lake Mariut

*T*his lake, which was once a vast basin, has decreased in size to a great degree, becoming a marshy zone with some picturesque spots where numerous birds come to nest.

Lake Mariut, called *Mareotis* in ancient times, is a vast swampland that extends south of

A dovecote at Lake Mariut

Alexandria and separates the Mediterranean coast from the desert. A narrow stretch of land

once separated the lake from nearby Lake Edku, situated east at Abusir (⇨ **41**). The Canopic arm of the Nile ran between these two basins, and Lake Mariut was connected to the river by a canal. This region therefore got much water from the Nile, especially during the flood period, and was quite fertile. It was also famous for its wine, which was praised both by Strabo in his *Geography* and the great Latin poets Catullus and Horace, which proves that the local wine was not drunk only in the region but was served at tables in Rome.

Major cities rose up at Lake Mariut: *Plinthine* and *Taposiris Magna* (⇨ **41**) on the northern bank, and *Philoxenite* (⇨ **40**) on the southern one. In the 19th century the lake began to grow smaller and, later, many

areas once under its waters were reclaimed to make room for civic and industrial

The shores of Lake Mariut are covered with thick vegetation of the genera Thipha *and* Phragmites

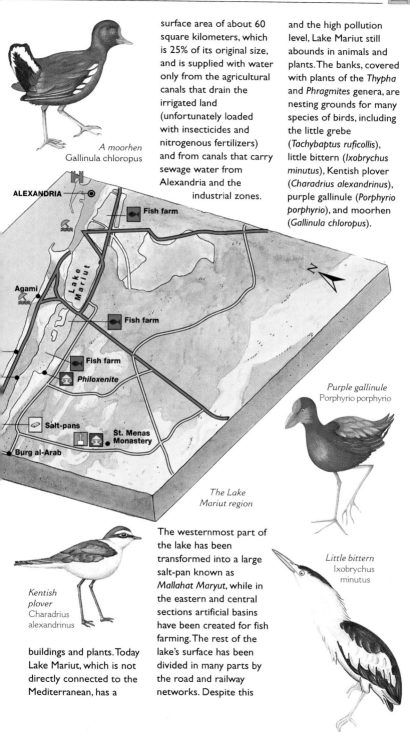

A moorhen
Gallinula chloropus

surface area of about 60 square kilometers, which is 25% of its original size, and is supplied with water only from the agricultural canals that drain the irrigated land (unfortunately loaded with insecticides and nitrogenous fertilizers) and from canals that carry sewage water from Alexandria and the industrial zones.

and the high pollution level, Lake Mariut still abounds in animals and plants. The banks, covered with plants of the *Thypha* and *Phragmites* genera, are nesting grounds for many species of birds, including the little grebe (*Tachybaptus ruficollis*), little bittern (*Ixobrychus minutus*), Kentish plover (*Charadrius alexandrinus*), purple gallinule (*Porphyrio porphyrio*), and moorhen (*Gallinula chloropus*).

ALEXANDRIA

Fish farm

Agami

L a k e   M a r i u t

Fish farm

Fish farm

Philoxenite

Salt-pans

St. Menas Monastery

Burg al-Arab

The Lake Mariut region

Purple gallinule
Porphyrio porphyrio

Kentish plover
Charadrius alexandrinus

The westernmost part of the lake has been transformed into a large salt-pan known as *Mallahat Maryut*, while in the eastern and central sections artificial basins have been created for fish farming. The rest of the lake's surface has been divided in many parts by the road and railway networks. Despite this

Little bittern
Ixobrychus minutus

buildings and plants. Today Lake Mariut, which is not directly connected to the Mediterranean, has a

Philoxenite

*F*ounded on the southern shore of Lake Mariut, the city of Philoxenite was a vast, rich city whose ruins are still quite impressive and fascinating.

View of the archaeological precinct of Philoxenite

The remains of the city of Philoxenite, sometimes erroneously called *Marea*, lie on the shore of Lake Mariut southeast of Abusir (⇨ **41**) and date from the 5th-6th century AD. This large and impressive site is easily recognizable from a distance because of an arch that was probably part of a construction housing a grain mill.

In fact, the city lay in a very fertile area, rich in cereals and grapevines, as is attested by the large wine press a few kilometers away. The remains of the port structures of Philoxenite are easy to spot, with their four large quays extending into the lake that must have been used to berth cargo ships or boats carrying pilgrims on their way to the nearby St. Menas Monastery (⇨ **42**).

The remains of a millstone at Philoxenite

Abusir

*T*he seaside town of Abusir has the only ancient lighthouse in Egypt. Although it was a funerary monument, the pharos can be considered a replica of the famous one in Alexandria.

Abusir, twenty kilometers west of Alexandria, corresponds to the ancient Greco-Roman site known as *Taposiris Magna*. Here, on a hilltop, there is a large Ptolemaic period temple dedicated to Osiris. The edifice was not finished and bears no inscriptions, yet its size is quite impressive: the enclosure walls are 100 meters long and 85 meters wide and, although in ruins, still have an average height of ten meters.

West of the temple is a large wall with a north-south alignment that must have served to force men and goods to make a detour through a customs checkpoint. Below this is an extremely interesting monument, a tomb crowned by a tower dating from Ptolemy II's reign (285–246 BC) that is nothing more or less than a miniature replica of the Alexandria pharos. The well-preserved structure clearly reveals three stories which are like those we see in the first- and second-century AD Alexandrian coins that represent the lighthouse in Alexandria. In fact, the Abusir funerary monument has a square first story, an

The Abusir funerary monument

octagonal second story, and a cylindrical third story. The locals called the monument *Burg al-Arab*, or "the Arab's Tower," the name also used later to indicate the present-day town in the vicinity.

The ruins of the unfinished Temple of Osiris

The St. Menas Monastery

*T*he ruins of the ancient monastery of St. Menas constitute a major archaeological site that has been included in the UNESCO World Heritage List.

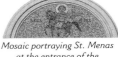

Mosaic portraying St. Menas at the entrance of the modern monastery

Overall view of the impressive remains of the St. Menas Monastery

The remains of the ancient monastery of St. Menas, also known as Abu Mina, are undoubtedly the least known Coptic monumental complex in Egypt, even though the site has been part of the UNESCO World Heritage List since

St. Menas (Coptic Museum, Cairo)

SAINT MENAS

According to tradition, Abu Mina or St. Menas was born in 275 in Phrygia (but more probably in Libya) to a family from the city of Nicopolis in the Delta that had converted to Christianity. Saint Menas enlisted in the Roman army, but during the persecution of Christians decreed by Diocletian he decided to desert and became a martyr in 296. His body was later transported to this desert site, where it was buried. At the behest of the patriarch Theophilos, the first sanctuary dedicated to him was built here. This saint, one of the most venerated in Egypt by the Copts, was credited with many miracles and his tomb became a pilgrimage site. To this day pilgrims come here to pray to St. Menas.

Typical terracotta flask used by pilgrims, decorated with the image of St. Menas (Greco-Roman Museum, Alexandria)

German archaeologist Carl Maria Kaufmann and the excavations, still in progress, are being carried out by the German Archaeological Institute of Cairo. The precinct includes the main basilica known as the Great Basilica, a martyrium, a baptistery,

seen. North of the Great Basilica are the baths, where the pilgrims not only went for their ablutions but also filled with the saint's "miraculous water" the typical two-handle terracotta flasks that were usually decorated with the image of St.

1979, on an equal footing with Islamic Cairo, the Giza pyramids, ancient Thebes, and the temple of Abu Simbel. The archaeological area is about two kilometers south of the modern monastery, which in turn is about ten kilometers south of the city of Burg al-Arab. Here lie the ruins of a large sanctuary whose golden age was the 5th and 6th centuries; it was pillaged in 836 by the caliph al-Mutasim, who was looking for marble, columns, and other prized building material to build his residence at Samarra, in Iraq. The site was discovered in 1905 by the

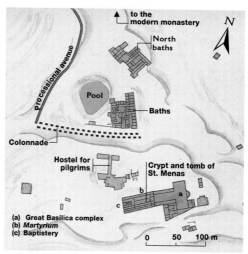

Plan of the St. Menas Monastery complex

baths, and the north and east basilicas. The Great Basilica was completed in the late 5th century by the emperor Zeno; it has a three-aisle nave and was the largest church in Egypt at that time. Immediately west of the basilica is the *martyrium*, consisting of a three-aisle church also known as the Small Basilica, under which is a crypt where the remains of the saint were laid. In the westernmost section is the 6th-century baptistery, impressive ruins of which can still be

Menas and were kept as precious relics. The large modern monastery, built in 1959 for the Patriarch Cyril VI, is a popular pilgrimage site.

One of the monks who live in the modern monastery of St. Menas

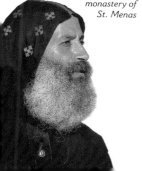

The St. Menas Monastery is one of the largest and most important in Egypt

Marina al-Alamein

This locality recently became a leading seaside resort, but thanks to excavations it has also taken on importance as an archaeological site.

View of the digs at Marina al-Alamein

Marina al-Alamein is a tourist village on the coast, 98 kilometers west of Alexandria. The beautiful beach and the clarity and color of the Mediterranean in this stretch of coastline have contributed to the great success of this locality. However, the site is also important from an archaeological standpoint, as research and digs carried out by a Polish mission have brought to light major ruins dating from a period from the end of the Ptolemaic age to the

A pillar in the recently excavated area

Roman age. These archaeologists found about one hundred tombs in the Marina al-Alamein necropolis, four of them carved out of the rock a few meters below ground level. The tombs in this site often have fairly well-preserved architectural elements on the exterior (columns or pillars) that

reveal the existence of external structures connected to funerary cults. In fact, the family of the deceased met in these pavilions to honor his/her memory. An in-depth study of the Marina al-Alamein necropolis will therefore certainly shed new light on Alexandrian funerary rituals.

One of the subterranean tombs discovered in the Marina al-Alamein necropolis

Al-Alamein

The Australian memorial

*T*his site was the theater of the decisive battle in North Africa during the Second World War and unforgettable memories of the conflict still echo here.

The Commonwealth military cemetery

A l-Alamein, on the edge of the Mediterranean about one hundred kilometers west of Alexandria, was the theater of a bloody World War Two battle between the Italian and German troops commanded by Field Marshal Edwin Rommel, and the Allied forces consisting of British and Commonwealth country troops. The twelve-day combat, from October 23 to November 4, 1942, proved decisive for control of North Africa. The memory of this terrible conflict, in which 68,500 soldiers lost their lives, is still fresh in this area, and a visit to Al-Alamein is doubtless a very moving experience.

The large Commonwealth Cemetery has rows and rows of 7,000 marble tombstones marking the graves of the British

The German military memorial

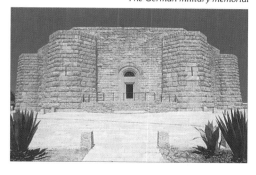

soldiers and their allies. In the immediate vicinity are monuments commemorating the Australians, Greeks, and South Africans who fought at their side. The remains of the German and Italian soldiers lie in two memorials built along the seaside a short distance farther west. The German military

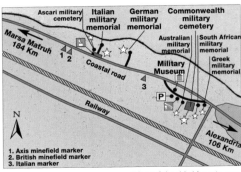

Plan of the Al-Alamein area

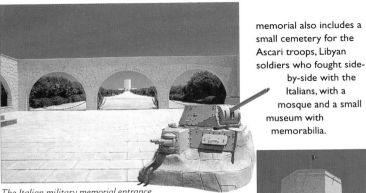

The Italian military memorial entrance

memorial also includes a small cemetery for the Ascari troops, Libyan soldiers who fought side-by-side with the Italians, with a mosque and a small museum with memorabilia.

memorial, seven kilometers from the Commonwealth cemetery, is an octagonal fortress in the middle of which is an obelisk; it contains the remains of 4,200 German soldiers that were placed there in 1958. About three

kilometers from here is the Italian military memorial, built in 1959. It consists of an octagonal tower in white Carrara marble housing the remains of 5,000 soldiers, 2,000 of whom have never been identified. This

The Italian military memorial

A heavy American Patton tank (Military Museum, Al-Alamein)

The Battle of Al-Alamein

At this locality, whose name means "the two hills," the combined German-Italian troops, made up of the *Afrika Korps* and eight Italian divisions, tried to reach Alexandria but were blocked by the British forces and their allies. Thus, the crafty circling maneuver planned by Rommel failed, and the battle ended on November 4, 1942 with a clear-cut

This marker, placed at the 111th km by the Italians, the furthermost advance point of the Axis forces, says: "Luck, not valour, was lacking."

THE BATTLE OF AL-ALAMEIN IN FIGURES

Date of the battle: October 23–November 4, 1942
Axis forces: 104,000 soldiers, 540 tanks, 2,433 cannons
Allied forces: 196,000 soldiers, 1,600 tanks, 3,171 cannons
Axis losses: 55,000 men, 1,000 cannons, 450 tanks
Allies' losses: 13,500 men, 100 cannons, 500 tanks

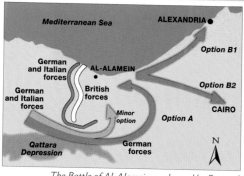

The Battle of Al-Alamein as planned by Rommel

General Montgomery (above left), the Allied commander, on the first page of the Daily Mirror describing the Battle of Al-Alamein

victory of the Allied troops headed by General Bernard L. Montgomery, who began their march eastward.

Field Marshal Erwin Rommel, the commander of the Axis troops

THE MILITARY MUSEUM

The Al-Alamein Military Museum provides a total, in-depth view of the war in North Africa. The museum, preceded by an outdoor section in which tanks and cannons are on exhibit, *has a fine collection of uniforms, weapons, and equipment used by both the Axis and Allied troops, as well as historic documents and a large model reconstruction of the Battle of Al-Alamein.*

ESSENTIAL BIBLIOGRAPHY

Chaveau M., *L'Égypte au temps de Cléopatre*, Paris, 1977.
Della Monica M., *Les derniers pharaons*, Paris, 1997.
Edwards J. (edited by), *Al-Alamein Revisited*, Cairo, 2000.
Empereur J.Y., *Alexandria Rediscovered*, London, 1998.
Empereur J.Y., *Le phare d'Alexandrie. La merveille retrouvée*, Paris, 1998.
Foreman L., *Cleopatra's Palace. In Search of a Legend*, London, 1999.
Forster E.N., *Alexandria. A History and a Guide*, Alexandria, 1922.
Fraser P.M., *Ptolemaic Alexandria*, Oxford, 1972.
La gloire d'Alexandrie, Paris, Catalogue de l'Exposition, Paris, 1998.
Tiersch, H., *Pharos, Antike Islam und Occident*, Leipzig, 1909.
Jobbins J., Megalli M., *The Egyptian Mediterranean. A Traveler's Guide*, Cairo, 1993.

PHOTOGRAPH CREDITS

All the photographs in this book are by Alberto Siliotti/Archivio Image Service-Geodia except for the following:

Stephane Compoint/Sygma: page 7 above.

Claudio Concina/Archivio Image Service - Geodia: pages 17 above, 20, 25 above, 30, 34, 35, 36, 44 below.

Franck Goddio/Hilti Foundation: page 33 above.

Bibliothèque Nationale de France, Paris: page 10 above and below.

DRAWINGS

All the drawings in this book are by Stefania Cossu except for the following:

Elisa Martini: birds of page 39.

Stefano Trainito: pages 24-25.